A Guide to
AMERICAN STATES

Virginia

THE OLD DOMINION

www.av2books.com

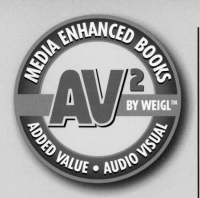

AV² provides enriched content that supplements and complements this book. Weigl's AV² books strive to create inspired learning and engage young minds in a total learning experience.

Your AV² Media Enhanced books come alive with...

Audio
Listen to sections of the book read aloud.

Key Words
Study vocabulary, and complete a matching word activity.

Video
Watch informative video clips.

Quizzes
Test your knowledge.

Embedded Weblinks
Gain additional information for research.

Slide Show
View images and captions, and prepare a presentation.

Try This!
Complete activities and hands-on experiments.

... and much, much more!

Go to **www.av2books.com**, and enter this book's unique code.

BOOK CODE

Z 9 7 8 0 4 4

AV² by Weigl brings you media enhanced books that support active learning.

Published by AV² by Weigl
350 5th Avenue, 59th Floor
New York, NY 10118
Website: www.av2books.com   www.weigl.com

Library of Congress Cataloging-in-Publication Data

Parker, Janice.
 Virginia / Janice Parker.
    p. cm. -- (A guide to American states)
 Includes index.
 ISBN 978-1-61690-819-5 (hardcover : alk. paper) -- ISBN 978-1-61690-495-1 (online)
 1. Virginia--Juvenile literature. I. Title.
 F226.3.P373 2011
 975.5--dc23
                                 2011019236

Printed in the United States of America in North Mankato, Minnesota

052011
WEP180511

Project Coordinator Jordan McGill
Art Director Terry Paulhus

Photo Credits
Every reasonable effort has been made to trace ownership and to obtain permission to reprint copyright material. The publishers would be pleased to have any errors or omissions brought to their attention so that they may be corrected in subsequent printings.

Weigl acknowledges Getty Images as its primary image supplier for this title.

Contents

Mount Vernon was an 8,000-acre estate when George Washington lived there in the 18ᵗʰ century. About 500 acres of the estate have been preserved as a museum and memorial to the nation's first president.

Introduction

A lthough Virginia is nicknamed the Old Dominion, it is often referred to as the "Birthplace of Presidents." Four of the first five U.S. presidents came from Virginia. George Washington, Thomas Jefferson, James Madison, and James Monroe all held the nation's highest office between 1789 and 1825.

Virginia played a crucial role in the American Revolution. Thomas Jefferson was responsible for writing the Declaration of Independence in 1776. Five years later, the decisive battle of the American Revolution was fought on Virginia soil, at Yorktown. During the siege of Yorktown, American and French troops led by General George Washington surrounded the British, who surrendered after 20 days. On June 25, 1788, Virginia became the tenth state to **ratify** the U.S. Constitution and join the Union.

Nicknamed "America's Favorite Drive," the scenic Blue Ridge Parkway extends from Shenandoah National Park in Virginia to the mountains of North Carolina.

The Hampton Roads region of southeastern Virginia builds and serves as a home port for U.S. Navy aircraft carriers.

Virginia **seceded** from the Union in April 1861. Richmond served as the capital of the Confederacy from June 1861 to April 1865, and much of the Civil War was fought on Virginia soil. Residents of Virginia's western counties had differing views from residents in the rest of the state. They had not wanted to leave the Union and voted to form a new state. One-third of Virginia became West Virginia in June 1863. The Confederate army led by Virginian Robert E. Lee surrendered to Union troops at Appomattox, Virginia, on April 9, 1865. Virginia was readmitted to the Union in January 1870.

Today, Virginia's economy is closely tied to that of the nation as a whole. A large and fast-growing part of the state's population lives in northeastern Virginia, in the Washington, D.C., **metropolitan area**. U.S. military bases and federal, state, and local governments in Virginia provide jobs for nearly one-fifth of the state's nonfarm labor force.

Where Is Virginia?

Virginia is located on the eastern coast of the United States. It is bordered by Maryland and Washington, D.C. to the northeast. Chesapeake Bay and the Atlantic Ocean are to the east. North Carolina and Tennessee are to the south. Kentucky is to the west, and West Virginia to the northwest.

The state has two major airports, both of which serve the Washington, D.C., area. Washington Dulles International Airport, in Chantilly, is one of the 50 busiest airports in the world and is especially important for service between the United States and Europe. The airport handles more than 23 million passengers each year. Ronald Reagan Washington National Airport, in Arlington, handles more than 18 million passengers annually.

Norfolk Southern operates more than 37,100 miles of railroad track and owns or leases nearly 4,000 locomotives and 90,000 freight cars.

Norfolk Southern, one of the world's largest rail freight companies, has its headquarters in Virginia. Amtrak provides the state with passenger rail service. Richmond is a transportation crossroads and the intersection point for two interstate highways, I-95 and I-64. Other interstate highways include I-66, which runs east-west, and I-77, I-81, and I-85, which run north-south. The Chesapeake Bay Bridge-Tunnel connects Virginia's Eastern Shore with the part of the state to the west of Chesapeake Bay. Ferry service is also available across the James River and Chesapeake Bay.

Construction of the Chesapeake Bay Bridge-Tunnel cost $200 million and took 42 months, from 1960 to 1964.

Mapping Virginia

Roughly triangular in shape, Virginia has a total area of 42,775 square miles. Land makes up about 93 percent of the total, and water accounts for the remaining 7 percent. Coastal waters make up more than half of the state's water area.

Virginia's coast is highly irregular. Including offshore islands, bays, and tidal areas of rivers and creeks, the state's shoreline measures 3,315 miles.

Sites and Symbols

STATE SEAL
Virginia

STATE BIRD
Cardinal

STATE FLOWER
Dogwood

STATE FLAG
Virginia

STATE INSECT
Tiger Swallowtail Butterfly

STATE TREE
Flowering Dogwood

Nickname The Old Dominion

Motto *Sic Semper Tyrannis* (Thus Ever to Tyrants)

Song no official state song

Entered the Union June 25, 1788, as the 10th state

Capital Richmond

Population (2010 Census) 8,001,024 Ranked 12th state

OHIO

Zanesville
Lancaster
Washington
Chillicothe
Athens
Marietta
Parkersburg
Portsmouth
Gallipolis
Maysville
Ironton
Morehead

KENTUCKY

Van Lear
Prestonsburg
Holden
Beckley
Madison
Princeton
Jenkins
Cumberland
Wise
Tazewell
Harlan
Marion
Bristol
Abingdon

Moundsville
Morgantown
Fairmont
Clarksburg
Philippi
Weston
Elkins

WEST VIRGINIA

Harrisonburg
Charleston
Huntington
Ripley

Lewisburg
Radford
Pulaski
Wytheville
Hillsville

PENNSYLVANIA

Cumberland
Keyser
Martinsburg

MARYLAND

Baltimore
Columbia
Annapolis
Winchester
Front Royal
Arlington
Alexandria
Washington
Woodbridge
Aquia Harbor
Fredericksburg
Charlottesville

Upper Darby
Wilmington
Glassboro
Vineland
Dover

DELAWARE

Easton
Salisbury
Pocomoke City

Staunton
Waynesboro
Clifton Forge
Buena Vista

VIRGINIA

Tuckahoe
Lynchburg
Richmond
Chester
Petersburg
Roanoke
Farmville
Christiansburg
Blackstone
Radford

Newport News
Hampton
Norfolk
Portsmouth
Chesapeake
Virginia Beach

ATLANTIC
OCEAN

Martinsville
Danville
South Hill
Emporia

TENNESSEE

Morristown
Boone
Cricket
Greensboro

NORTH CAROLINA

Map Scale

0   100 Miles

N

STATE CAPITAL

Jamestown was Virginia's seat of government from 1619 to 1699, when the capital was moved to Williamsburg. Located on the James River, Richmond has been the capital of Virginia since 1780. It also served as the capital of the Confederacy during the Civil War. Today, Richmond has more than 204,000 residents and is Virginia's fifth-largest city.

United States

Hawai'i   Alaska

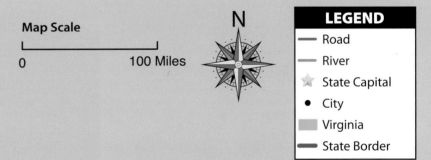

Virginia

The Land

Virginia consists of several distinct regions. The Eastern Shore, at the southern tip of the Delmarva Peninsula, is separated from the rest of Virginia by Chesapeake Bay. Extending inland from the coast is the Coastal Plain, a flat and swampy region. This area is sometimes called the Tidewater.

West of the Coastal Plain is the Piedmont. This region has low, rolling hills and fertile soils. The Blue Ridge region is made up of mountains that form a ridge crossing the state from northeast to southwest. West of the Blue Ridge lies the Ridge and Valley region and another mountainous area, the Appalachian Plateau. Both the Blue Ridge and the Appalachian Plateau are parts of the larger Appalachian Mountain chain.

POTOMAC RIVER

The Potomac River separates Arlington, Virginia, from Washington, D.C.

SHENANDOAH NATIONAL PARK

Located in northern Virginia, Shenandoah National Park includes the 4,050-foot-high summit of Hawksbill Mountain.

CHESAPEAKE BAY

Chesapeake Bay extends about 200 miles from Havre de Grace, Maryland, to Virginia Beach. The bay has a surface area of nearly 4,500 square miles.

SMITH MOUNTAIN LAKE

Smith Mountain Lake was developed by a power company to provide electricity, drinking water, and recreational opportunities for surrounding areas of southwestern Virginia.

The Delmarva Peninsula got its name from the three states of Delaware, Maryland, and Virginia. Part of the peninsula is in each of those states.

Ranked by size, Virginia is the 35th largest of the 50 states in total area.

Mount Rogers is the highest point in Virginia, with an altitude of 5,729 feet.

The Rappahannock River rises in the Blue Ridge Mountains and empties into Chesapearke Bay. Other important rivers in Virginia include the James, the Potomac, and the Shenandoah.

Lake Drummond covers about 3,140 acres and is the largest natural lake in Virginia. It is located in the center of the Great Dismal Swamp. The lake has a maximum depth of only 6 feet.

Created in the early 1960s, Smith Mountain Lake has an area of more than 20,000 acres. This artificial lake has an average depth of 55 feet and a maximum depth of 250 feet.

Hurricane Isabel in September 2003 downed many trees and power lines. The storm caused at least $1.6 billion in property damage and left more than 2 million households without electricity.

Climate

While Virginia generally has hot, humid summers and mild, wet winters, the climate varies across the state. Southeastern Virginia, near the coast, has a mild climate with very little snowfall. The northwestern part of the state has colder winters, with greater snowfall in elevated areas.

Average temperatures in Richmond range from 36° Fahrenheit in January to 78° F in July. Record temperatures in the state include a high of 110° F in 1954 and a low of –30° F in 1985.

Average Annual Temperatures Across Virginia

Temperatures in Norfolk average nearly 10° F warmer than those in Blacksburg. What geographical factors account for the difference?

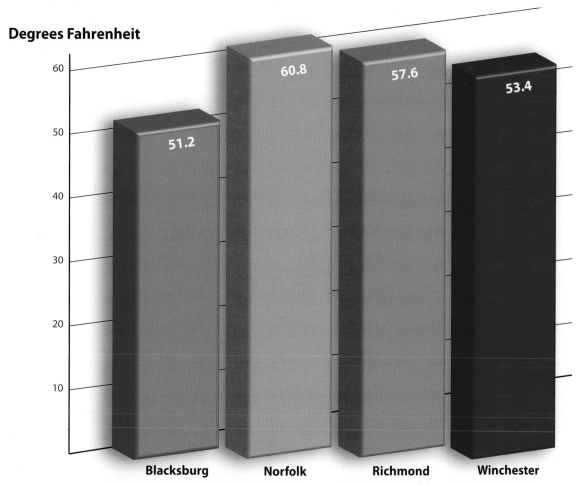

Degrees Fahrenheit

Blacksburg	Norfolk	Richmond	Winchester
51.2	60.8	57.6	53.4

Natural Resources

Virginia's rich soils have helped to make agriculture a primary industry. The tobacco industry was crucial to the success of the Virginia colony, which might not have survived without the revenue that tobacco sales produced. Tobacco growing and the manufacturing of tobacco products have declined in recent decades, but they still make a notable contribution to the state economy.

At a reconstruction of the Jamestown settlement, a historical interpreter demonstrates how the early settlers cultivated tobacco.

Annual production of nonfuel minerals is worth more than $1 billion. Crushed stone and other construction materials account for most of the output. The Old Dominion also produces about 30 million tons of coal per year. Virginia companies manufacture lumber, furniture, flooring, paper, and other wood products from the state's extensive forest resources. More than 60 percent of the state's land area is classified as commercially productive woodland.

At Norfolk Southern's Lamberts Point pier in Norfolk, coal mined in Virginia and elsewhere is loaded for shipment overseas.

Plants

Hardwood trees such as hickories, maples, white oaks, and red oaks are abundant in Virginia's forests. Other trees commonly found in the Old Dominion include white pines, sycamores, and willows. In the wetlands, tupelos, bald cypresses, and swamp oaks grow. Dogwood can be found throughout most of the state, while azaleas, mountain laurels, and rhododendrons are common in the mountain regions.

The Virginia Native Plant Society was founded in 1982 to help conserve plants that are native to the state. The society also chooses a wildflower of the year. One popular wildflower is the trailing arbutus, commonly known as the mayflower.

KUDZU

Introduced from Japan in the late 19th century to control erosion, kudzu vines can grow up to 1 foot per day, crowding out other vegetation.

TUPELO

Prized for its fiery red color in autumn, the tupelo tree is also valuable as a source of pulp for paper and wood for carvers.

HICKORY

The hard, strong wood of the hickory tree is used for baseball bats, skis, and tool handles, among other products.

MAYFLOWER

The mayflower, or trailing arbutus, is a small evergreen shrub that grows in forested areas.

The dogwood was adopted as the official state flower in 1918. In 1956, the dogwood was also declared the state tree.

Kudzu is a common sight throughout Virginia, especially along roadsides. It also grows in vacant or abandoned properties.

Wildflowers such as windflowers, geraniums, asters, and trilliums are colorful additions to the Virginia countryside.

According to the U.S. Fish and Wildlife Service, there are 15 species of plants in Virginia that are either **endangered** or **threatened**. These include the eastern prairie fringed orchid and the Virginia round-leaf birch.

Animals

Although many large mammals once lived in Virginia, only the black bear and the white-tailed deer still roam the state. Smaller mammals such as beavers, muskrats, skunks, otters, foxes, and raccoons are more plentiful. Common reptiles and **amphibians** include the box turtle and the bullfrog. More than 30 species of snakes, including the eastern garter snake, live in Virginia. Poisonous snakes include the timber rattlesnake, the northern copperhead, and the eastern cottonmouth.

Virginia is located along the path of the Atlantic Flyway. The flyway is a route for migrating birds that runs along the eastern coast of North America. Migrating ducks and geese take advantage of the many rivers and marshes in the state. During summer, warblers and orioles live in Virginia. Nuthatches and woodpeckers live in the state's forests, while gulls, herons, and bitterns reside around lakes and ponds. Birds of prey that live in the state include the bald eagle, the peregrine falcon, and the osprey.

WHITE-TAILED DEER

Wildlife management efforts have succeeded in boosting Virginia's deer population from an estimated 150,000 in 1950 to nearly 1 million in recent years.

BEAVER

Found throughout Virginia, especially where aspen trees are plentiful, beavers prefer smooth-bottomed streams to ones that are steep and rocky.

NORTHERN COPPERHEAD

The poisonous northern copperhead occurs throughout the state at elevations below 3,000 feet.

CARDINAL

Found throughout the state, the cardinal has also been called the "Virginia red bird" and the "Virginia nightingale."

The American foxhound is the state dog. George Washington first brought foxhounds into Virginia to hunt foxes.

The state shell has been the oyster since 1974.

Many species of whales can be found off the coast of Virginia, including humpback and fin whales.

The cardinal became Virginia's official state bird in 1950.

The tiger swallowtail butterfly is the state insect.

More than 50 animals are on the U.S. Fish and Wildlife Service's Threatened and Endangered Species list for Virginia. One of the endangered species is the Virginia big-eared bat, the official state bat.

Tourism

The beauty of Virginia Beach once prompted an early explorer to exclaim, "Heaven and Earth never agreed better to frame a place for man's **habitations** than Virginia." Today, Virginia Beach is not only the largest city in the state but also one of the most popular resorts on the East Coast.

One of Virginia's most treasured sites is Monticello, the home of Thomas Jefferson. For more than 40 years, Jefferson built and rebuilt the house into one of the most impressive homes in the world. Another popular attraction is George Washington's home, Mount Vernon.

Tourists are also drawn to Virginia's many historic attractions. Battlefields from the American Revolution and the Civil War are scattered across the state. Colonial Williamsburg attracts more than 680,000 paying customers per year. Many of the village's buildings and streets have been restored to their 18th-century splendor.

VIRGINIA BEACH

More than 2.7 million people per year visit Virginia Beach.

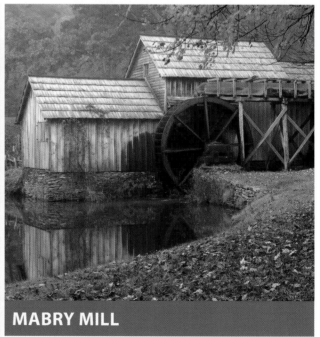

MABRY MILL

Located along the Blue Ridge Parkway, Mabry Mill features a working, water-powered grist mill and demonstrations of old-time Appalachian crafts.

COLONIAL WILLIAMSBURG

Dedicated in 1934, the restored House of Burgesses is the centerpiece of Colonial Williamsburg. Virginia's legislature continues to meet here instead of Richmond on special ceremonial occasions.

ARLINGTON NATIONAL CEMETERY

Each year, about 6,900 military veterans and others are honored with burial at Arlington National Cemetery.

Industry

Agriculture was once the dominant industry in Virginia. Today, it contributes less than 1 percent to the state economy. Principal agricultural products include **broiler chickens**, eggs, cattle, greenhouse or nursery goods, milk, fodder crops, tobacco, turkeys, and peanuts.

Industries in Virginia
Value of Goods and Services in Millions of Dollars

In 1800, the federal and state governments were very small, and agriculture was Virginia's main economic activity. How has the state economy changed since that time?

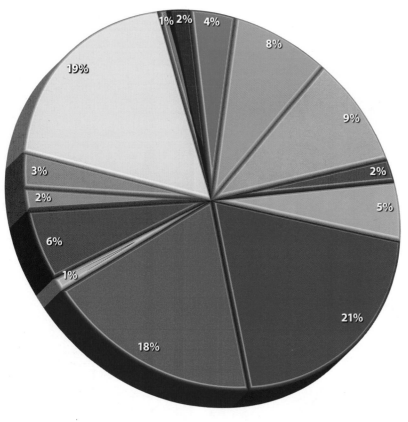

LEGEND

*	Agriculture, Forestry, and Fishing	$1,252
	Mining	$2,123
	Utilities	$6,326
	Construction	$15,372
	Manufacturing	$30,866
	Wholesale and Retail Trade	$36,694
	Transportation	$8,985
	Media and Entertainment	$21,447
	Finance, Insurance, and Real Estate	$85,829
	Professional and Technical Services	$73,042
	Education	$3,718
	Health Care	$23,882
	Hotels and Restaurants	$9,418
	Other Services	$10,757
	Government	$76,594
	TOTAL	**$406,305**

*Less than 1%. Percentages may not add to 100 because of rounding.

Chesapeake Bay provides Virginia with many different types of fish. More than 200 million clams and nearly 5 million oysters are harvested annually. Crabs, sea scallops, flounder, and striped bass are also important to commercial fishing in the state.

Traditionally, tobacco products were among Virginia's most valuable manufactured goods. Today, the state also makes electronic components, chemical products, processed foods, clothing, transportation equipment, and furniture, as well as other wood products. Virginia's top exports include machinery, coal, transportation equipment, plastics, paper, optical and medical instruments, and chemicals.

Virginia has about 47,000 farms. Together they cover some 8 million acres.

Goods and Services

The federal government employs many Virginians and is essential to the state's economy. The Pentagon in Arlington is the headquarters of the U.S. Department of Defense and is one of the largest office buildings in the world. The department employs about 23,000 military and **civilian** workers. They receive support from another 3,000 people who work at the site in nondefense jobs.

Although the Pentagon contains 17.5 miles of hallways, it takes no more than seven minutes to walk between any two points in the building.

Many important military bases are located in Virginia, including the world's largest naval station, at Norfolk. The U.S. Marine Corps Base in Quantico is where all U.S. Marines receive their basic training. The Quantico facility also hosts the training academy of the Federal Bureau of Investigation, or FBI.

The Library of Virginia, in Richmond, contains the **archives** of the Commonwealth of Virginia. Leading public colleges and universities in the state include the University of Virginia in Charlottesville, Virginia Tech in Blacksburg, and the College of William and Mary in Williamsburg. Founded in 1839, the state-supported Virginia Military Institute is located in Lexington.

The Virginia Military Institute, or VMI, enrolls 1,500 male and female cadets. Women have been admitted since 1997.

I DIDN'T KNOW THAT!

On September 11, 2001, a **hijacked** commercial jetliner crashed into the Pentagon, causing part of it to collapse. More than 180 people were killed. The crash was part of a terrorist attack on the United States that also resulted in the destruction of the Twin Towers of the World Trade Center in New York City. The Pentagon quickly recovered from the attack.

Virginia's first newspaper was the *Gazette*, which began publication in Williamsburg in 1736.

When the Syms Free School in Hampton was founded in 1634, it became the first free public school in the United States.

The Central Intelligence Agency, or CIA, has its headquarters at Langley, which is part of McLean in Fairfax County.

American Indians

Prehistoric Indians lived in the Virginia region at least 16,000 years ago. These early peoples used tools made of stone and relied mainly on hunting for their food. About 3,000 years ago, some groups began to settle in villages. They hunted, fished, and grew food crops such as corn and squash, as well as tobacco. They made ceramic bowls and other pottery, and they traded with nearby groups.

Probably about 50,000 American Indians were living in the region by the 1600s, when the first European settlers arrived. These Indians mostly spoke languages belonging to the Algonquian, Iroquoian, and Siouan language groups.

Pocahontas was baptized and given the European name Rebecca before she married the English settler John Rolfe.

Early European settlers came in contact with Indians of the Powhatan Confederacy, which included at least 30 Algonquian-speaking groups that lived near the coast. The confederacy had been founded by and was named for a powerful chief, Powhatan.

Violence erupted between settlers and Indians, and in 1613 the English colonists captured Powhatan's daughter, Pocahontas. She eventually married an English settler, John Rolfe. The marriage brought peace to the area for several years. Fighting resumed between the Powhatan Confederacy and the English a few years after her death in 1617.

At Jamestown, historical interpreters show how the Powhatan Indians performed such tasks as tanning animal hides.

A replica of the Susan Constant docked at Jamestown during ceremonies marking the 400th anniversary of the founding of the English colony.

Explorers

S ailing for England, John Cabot may have been the first European to see Virginia when he reached North America in 1497. In 1524, the Italian explorer Giovanni da Verrazzano explored Virginia's coast for France.

In 1606, three ships carrying 104 passengers from the Virginia Company of London traveled from England to North America. The Virginia Company had been created to settle Virginia. After arriving in May 1607, the voyagers on the *Susan Constant, Godspeed*, and *Discovery* founded a settlement called Jamestown. Conflict with the Powhatan Indians, along with a drought, made life difficult for the colonists, and many starved to death.

When Sir Thomas Gates arrived in Jamestown in 1610 to become governor of the colony, he found only 60 surviving settlers. Just as the settlers were about to abandon the colony, Sir Thomas West, baron de la Warr, arrived and took control of the Jamestown settlement. Gradually, life in Jamestown began to improve.

Timeline of Settlement

Early Exploration and Settlement

1524 Sailing for France, Italian navigator Giovanni da Verrazzano explores the Virginia coastline.

1607 English settlers found a colony at Jamestown.

1619 An elected legislature, the House of Burgesses, begins meeting. The first shipload of Africans arrives.

Further Colonization

1676 Colonial authorities put down Bacon's Rebellion, a settler uprising.

1693 Virginia's first college, the College of William and Mary, is founded in Williamsburg.

1699 Williamsburg becomes Virginia's colonial capital.

Independence and American Revolution

1775 Early in the American Revolution, George Washington, a Virginian, becomes commander-in-chief of the Continental Army.

1776 Another Virginian, Thomas Jefferson, drafts the Declaration of Independence.

1781 The defeat of the British at Yorktown secures an American victory in the Revolutionary War.

Statehood and Civil War

1788 Virginia is the 10th state to ratify the Constitution and join the Union.

1789–1825 Four of the nation's first five presidents, including Washington and Jefferson, are Virginians.

1861–1865 Virginia secedes from the Union, and Richmond becomes the capital of the Confederacy. The Civil War ends with Confederate General Robert E. Lee's surrender at Appomattox.

Early Settlers

C olonial Virginia was built on tobacco. American Indian groups had been using tobacco as a medicine and in ceremonies for at least 2,000 years. John Rolfe, a colonist who came to Virginia in 1610, began to grow a type of tobacco from the West Indies that had a mild taste. Growers in Virginia exported it to England and the rest of Europe, where it became very popular.

Map of Settlements and Resources in Early Virginia

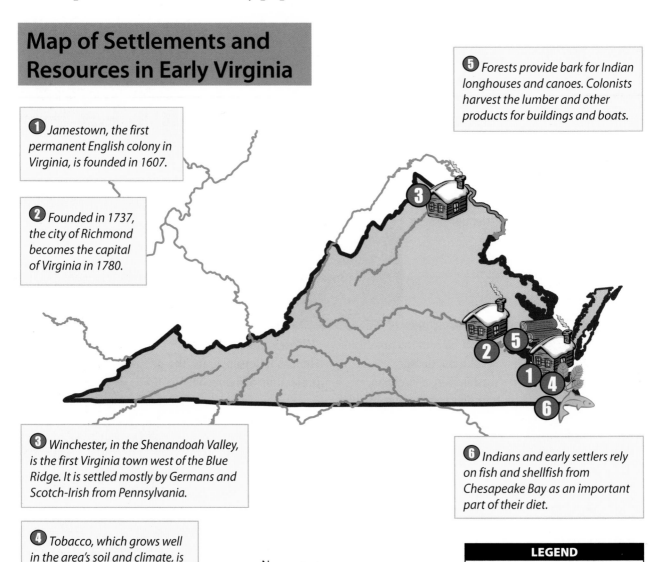

5 Forests provide bark for Indian longhouses and canoes. Colonists harvest the lumber and other products for buildings and boats.

1 Jamestown, the first permanent English colony in Virginia, is founded in 1607.

2 Founded in 1737, the city of Richmond becomes the capital of Virginia in 1780.

3 Winchester, in the Shenandoah Valley, is the first Virginia town west of the Blue Ridge. It is settled mostly by Germans and Scotch-Irish from Pennsylvania.

6 Indians and early settlers rely on fish and shellfish from Chesapeake Bay as an important part of their diet.

4 Tobacco, which grows well in the area's soil and climate, is the Jamestown colony's most important cash crop and becomes the mainstay of Virginia's agriculture.

N

Scale

0   100 Miles

LEGEND

Settlement	Tobacco
River	Virginia
Fish	State Border
Wood	

Packed in barrels, the first shipload of tobacco left Virginia for England in 1614.

The settlement soon began to thrive. By 1619, it had its own government, with a two-chamber legislature. In 1624, Virginia became a royal colony.

Black Africans were first brought to Jamestown in 1619 as **indentured servants**. Legalized slavery was not introduced for several decades. Black slaves were the foundation of the **plantation** agriculture that began in the Tidewater region and spread into the Piedmont.

In 1676, a group of settlers led by the English aristocrat and colonist Nathaniel Bacon rose up against Virginia's colonial government in what is known as Bacon's Rebellion. The group opposed many of Governor William Berkeley's policies. They disliked the governor's refusal to call elections, his lack of a plan to combat Indian attacks, and his favoritism toward new, wealthy colonists. The rebels attacked and burned Jamestown, forcing Berkeley to flee. When Bacon died unexpectedly, Berkeley returned, reclaimed power, and hanged many of the rebels without trials.

I DIDN'T KNOW THAT!

Sir Thomas Gates's ship was hit by a hurricane on the way to Virginia. He and his men had to spend the winter in Bermuda before finally making their way to the colony in 1610.

Explorers from the Virginia Company of London sailed into a river they named the James River, after King James I of England. Jamestown was also named after the king.

The colonists called the winter of 1609–1610 the "Starving Time" because so many settlers died of starvation or illness.

After the death of Pocahontas and her father, Powhatan, the Powhatan Indians killed about 350 colonists during what is called the Great Massacre of 1622. In 1644, the Powhatans attacked the Virginia colony, killing about 500 settlers. In a peace agreement the Powhatans agreed to move north of the James and York rivers, and eventually they moved westward.

The House of Burgesses, a branch of Virginia's early government, was the first elected legislative body in North America.

Notable People

More than any other state, Virginia provided the talented and courageous leaders who transformed the original 13 colonies into a free and independent nation. More recently, inspirational educators, creative musical artists, and pioneering athletes have called Virginia their home.

GEORGE WASHINGTON (1732–1799)

Born in Westmoreland County, George Washington is celebrated as the "Father of His Country." Trained as a farmer, surveyor, and soldier, he served with the British Army in the 1750s but later became a strong supporter of American independence. He commanded the Continental Army during the American Revolution. Later, he presided over the convention that in 1787 drafted the U.S. Constitution, the nation's founding document. The country's first president, he served two terms, from 1789 to 1797, before retiring to his home in Mount Vernon. Washington, D.C., and the state of Washington are named for him.

THOMAS JEFFERSON (1743–1826)

A native of Albermarle County, Thomas Jefferson was only 33 years old in 1776 when he wrote the Declaration of Independence. He also served as governor of Virginia, U.S. ambassador to France, and U.S. secretary of state. After four years as vice president under President John Adams, he defeated Adams in 1800 to become the third U.S. president. He held the presidency from 1801 to 1809. During that time, the nation greatly expanded its territory through the Louisiana Purchase of 1803. Like the other Virginia "founding fathers," Jefferson had doubts about slavery but continued to own slaves until the end of his life.

JAMES MADISON
(1751–1836)

The son of a Virginia tobacco planter, James Madison grew up to become one of the 18th century's greatest political thinkers. Known as the "Father of the Constitution," he had a major role in writing and explaining the nation's founding document. He served from 1809 to 1817 as the fourth U.S. president, leading the country through the War of 1812.

JAMES MONROE
(1758–1831)

A lawyer, legislator, and follower of Thomas Jefferson, James Monroe served as the nation's fifth president, from 1817 to 1825. Monroe famously declared that the United States would resist any future efforts by Europe to colonize or interfere with countries of the Americas.

BOOKER T. WASHINGTON
(1856–1915)

Born a slave in southwestern Virginia, Booker T. Washington became an influential educator and African American leader. He believed education for freed slaves should emphasize the practical skills they needed to advance economically. His book *Up from Slavery* was so well regarded that he was invited to dinner at the White House.

I DIDN'T KNOW THAT!

Ella Fitzgerald (1917–1996) ranks among the greatest jazz singers of all time. As a big-band singer and recording artist, she excelled at interpreting the works of American composers such as Cole Porter, Duke Ellington, and Irving Berlin. She also specialized in "scat singing," using her voice to improvise wordlessly, as a solo jazz player might use a horn.

Arthur Ashe (1943–1993) was born and raised in Richmond, where he showed early tennis talent. He went on to become a college tennis champion and was the first African American man to win the U.S. Open and Wimbledon tennis titles. He entered the International Tennis Hall of Fame in 1985.

Population

T he 2010 Census counted more than 8 million people in the Old Dominion. The state population grew by 13 percent between 2000 and 2010. Growth was especially rapid in northern Virginia, which includes the counties near Washington, D.C. This region, which is home to one of every four Virginia residents, experienced a 23 percent population increase during the decade.

Virginia Population 1950–2010

The northern Virginia region has been growing much more rapidly than the state as a whole. How can the state government provide essential services to this region's expanding population without neglecting the needs of the rest of the state?

Number of People

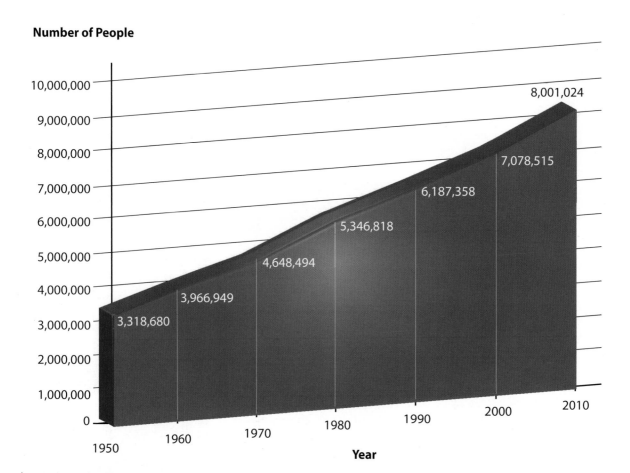

1950	3,318,680
1960	3,966,949
1970	4,648,494
1980	5,346,818
1990	6,187,358
2000	7,078,515
2010	8,001,024

Year

Almost three-fourths of the state's population is of European ancestry. Many people have British, German, or Irish heritage. The state has a higher percentage of African Americans than the national average and a smaller proportion of Hispanic Americans.

More than seven of every 10 Virginians live in cities or towns. Some of these places are part of the Washington, D.C., metropolitan area. The state has a highly educated workforce. Approximately 82 percent of Virginians over the age of 25 are high school graduates. About 30 percent of the state's citizens have a college or university degree.

With a resident population of more than 43,000, the city of Charlottesville is the home of the University of Virginia. The university enrolls more than 20,000 students annually.

Politics and Government

Virginia's constitution divides the state government into executive, legislative, and judicial branches. The head of the executive branch is the governor, who is elected to a single four-year term and may not run for reelection. The governor has the power to approve or **veto** state laws. Other elected executive officials include the lieutenant governor and the attorney general, both of whom may serve an unlimited number of four-year terms.

Richmond, the capital of Virginia, is the center of a metropolitan area with more than 1.2 million people.

The General Assembly is the state's lawmaking body, or legislature. It consists of the House of Delegates, with 100 members, and the Senate, with 40 members. Delegates are elected for two-year terms, and senators are elected for four-year terms. The judicial branch is the state's court system. The highest court is the Supreme Court. It consists of a chief justice and six other justices.

Virginia has 95 counties and 39 cities that are independent of county government. The state sends 11 representatives and two senators to the U.S. Congress. Virginia casts 13 electoral votes in presidential elections.

John Warner, a Republican, served as secretary of the Navy in the early 1970s. He held office for 30 years as a U.S. senator from Virginia before resuming his career as a lawyer in 2009.

The state seal features a woman representing virtue. The woman holds both a sword and a spear. Her left foot rests on a figure, representing tyranny, lying on the ground. The seal was adopted in 1776.

Virginia does not have an official state song. "Carry Me Back to Ol' Virginny," written by James A. Bland, was the state song from 1940 through the mid-1990s. Many people came to regard the racial language and attitudes in the song as outdated and offensive. In 1997, the General Assembly voted to make it "state song emeritus." This meant that the song, while honored for its history, would be retired and no longer played on public occasions.

Eight men born in Virginia have become U.S. presidents. The eight are George Washington, Thomas Jefferson, James Madison, James Monroe, William Henry Harrison, John Tyler, Zachary Taylor, and Woodrow Wilson.

Cultural Groups

The first Africans arrived in the Virginia colony in 1619. The expansion of tobacco growing in the colony led to a rise in the demand for African slave labor. By 1860, on the eve of the Civil War, nearly 500,000 African American slaves were living in the state. The war put an end to slavery, but the state passed new laws intended to make African Americans legally and economically inferior to whites.

In the 1950s, when the U.S. Supreme Court outlawed racially **segregated** public schools, many public schools in the Old Dominion were closed in order to prevent white and black Virginians from going to school together. After some years, the state dropped this policy of "massive resistance," and school segregation ended. In 1989, state voters elected Virginia's first African American governor, Douglas Wilder. Each February, during Black History Month, many events throughout the state recall the history of African Americans in Virginia, as well as African American contributions to the early history of the nation.

Born in Richmond, Douglas Wilder was the first African American in U.S. history to win a statewide election for governor.

At Yorktown High School in Arlington, immigrant students collaborate on essays and poems that describe their experience in coming to the United States. Arlington's percentage of foreign-born residents is more than three times higher than that of the state as a whole.

Many Virginia festivals celebrate the state's colonial history and the lives of the early European settlers. The Frontier Culture Museum near Staunton has exhibits that show what life was like for the early settlers. The Virginia First Thanksgiving Festival is held each year at Berkeley Plantation and features re-creations of the original celebration, including crafts, music, and food.

American Indian culture is celebrated throughout Virginia. Each May, Clarksville is the site of the annual Native American Heritage Festival and Powwow. It features American Indian arts, songs, and dances.

Arts and Entertainment

The arts have a long history of support in Virginia. The state-supported Virginia Museum of Fine Arts opened in Richmond in 1936. Virginia's capital city also has a symphony orchestra and a ballet company. The Virginia Opera presents productions in Richmond, Norfolk, and Fairfax. One of the state's newest museums is the Taubman Museum of Art in Roanoke. Notable theaters in Virginia include the Barter Theatre in Abingdon and the American Shakespeare Center in Staunton.

Virginia has produced many well-known writers. The Pulitzer Prize–winning novelist Willa Cather was born near Winchester. Her works include *O Pioneers!, My Antonia, One of Ours*, and *Death Comes for the Archbishop*. Tom Wolfe, a Richmond native, wrote acclaimed works such as *The Bonfire of the Vanities* and *The Right Stuff*.

Tom Wolfe's history of the early U.S. space program, The Right Stuff, won a National Book Award.

Pearl Bailey achieved one of her biggest successes with the starring role in an all-African American version of the Broadway musical Hello, Dolly!

Two talented female vocalists had ties to Newport News. Jazz singer Ella Fitzgerald was internationally known as the "First Lady of Song," while Pearl Bailey became known as a star of stage, screen, and nightclubs. Winchester was the home city of Patsy Cline, an all-time great in the field of country music. Cline was the first female solo performer to enter the Country Music Hall of Fame. The Carter Family and Roy Clark are two other famous country music acts from Virginia. Many famous bluegrass musicians are associated with the state, including the Virginia-born singer, banjo player, and bandleader Ralph Stanley.

Patsy Cline's music has continued to influence other country singers long after her death in a plane crash in 1963.

Bruce Hornsby, a singer, songwriter, and keyboard player, was born in Williamsburg.

The Barter Theatre, in Abingdon, accepted food, instead of money, for admission to performances during the Great Depression of the 1930s. This was a time of economic hardship for the whole country.

The Virginia Symphony was founded in 1920 and performs regularly in the Hampton Roads area and Williamsburg.

The Edgar Allan Poe Museum opened in Richmond in 1922 to document and celebrate the writer's life.

William Styron, author of the acclaimed novels *The Confessions of Nat Turner* and *Sophie's Choice*, was born in Newport News in 1925.

Film stars Warren Beatty and Shirley MacLaine were born in Richmond. Beatty, who is MacLaine's younger brother, is also an award-winning movie director.

Sports

Virginia's rivers, lakes, forests, mountains, and coastal areas offer a variety of recreational opportunities. Camping, hiking, hunting, boating, and fishing are popular in the state, especially in national forests and state parks. Lake Anna and Smith Mountain Lake cater to boating enthusiasts, while the James, Shenandoah, and Maury rivers attract kayakers and canoeists. Fishers need licenses to catch the many varieties of bass, trout, pike, and other freshwater fish in the state. Virginia is also an excellent location for saltwater fishing.

Whitewater on the Potomac River at Great Falls Park ranges from the moderately easy Class 2 all the way up to the extremely challenging Class 6.

Several former rail routes have been adapted for use by hikers, cyclists, and horseback riders. The New River Trail is a 52-mile rail bed between Galax and Pulaski, and the Virginia Creeper Trail, between Abingdon and Whitetop, is 34 miles long. Hikers also use the 550-mile portion of the Appalachian Trail that winds through Virginia. Downhill skiing in Virginia is available at the Homestead, Bryce, Massanutten, and Wintergreen resorts. During the summer, Bryce Resort, in the Shenandoah Valley, also offers grass skiing and mountain boarding. Grass skiing actually uses skates instead of skis, and mountain boarding is like snowboarding on wheels.

Both recreational and competitive horseback riding are well established in Virginia. Every year, **steeplechase** fans watch to see who will win the Virginia Gold Cup Races. NASCAR fans head for stock-car auto racetracks at Richmond and Martinsville. In college sports, the Hokies of Virginia Tech have a wide following.

The Great Meadow steeplechase course in The Plains, Virginia, hosts the Virginia Gold Cup and International Gold Cup races.

National Averages Comparison

The United States is a federal republic, consisting of fifty states and the District of Columbia. Alaska and Hawai'i are the only non-contiguous, or non-touching, states in the nation. Today, the United States of America is the third-largest country in the world in population. The United States Census Bureau takes a census, or count of all the people, every ten years. It also regularly collects other kinds of data about the population and the economy. How does Virginia compare to the national average?

Comparison Chart

United States 2010 Census Data *	USA	Virginia
Admission to Union	NA	June 25, 1788
Land Area (in square miles)	3,537,438.44	39,594.07
Population Total	308,745,538	8,001,024
Population Density (people per square mile)	87.28	202.08
Population Percentage Change (April 1, 2000, to April 1, 2010)	9.7%	13.0%
White Persons (percent)	72.4%	68.6%
Black Persons (percent)	12.6%	19.4%
American Indian and Alaska Native Persons (percent)	0.9%	0.4%
Asian Persons (percent)	4.8%	5.5%
Native Hawaiian and Other Pacific Islander Persons (percent)	0.2%	0.1%
Some Other Race (percent)	6.2%	3.2%
Persons Reporting Two or More Races (percent)	2.9%	2.9%
Persons of Hispanic or Latino Origin (percent)	16.3%	7.9%
Not of Hispanic or Latino Origin (percent)	83.7%	92.1%
Median Household Income	$52,029	$61,210
Percentage of People Age 25 or Over Who Have Graduated from High School	80.4%	81.5%

*All figures are based on the 2010 United States Census, with the exception of the last two items. Percentages may not add to 100 because of rounding.

How to Improve My Community

S trong communities make strong states. Think about what features are important in your community. What do you value? Education? Health? Forests? Safety? Beautiful spaces? Government works to help citizens create ideal living conditions that are fair to all by providing services in communities. Consider what changes you could make in your community. How would they improve your state as a whole? Using this concept web as a guide, write a report that outlines the features you think are most important in your community and what improvements could be made. A strong state needs strong communities.

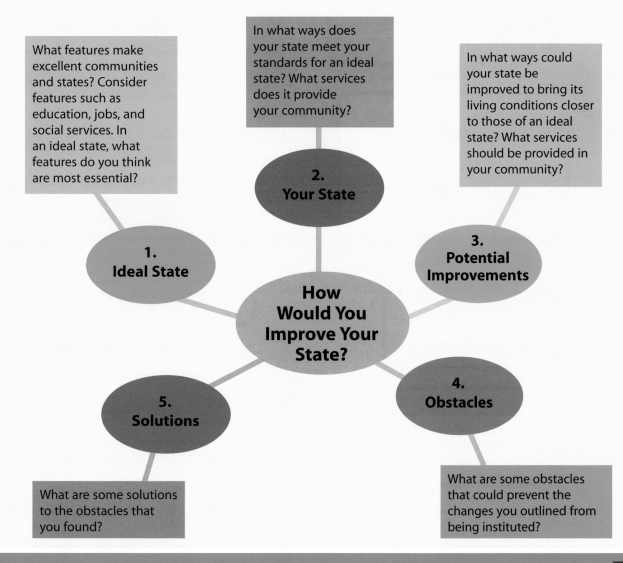

What features make excellent communities and states? Consider features such as education, jobs, and social services. In an ideal state, what features do you think are most essential?

In what ways does your state meet your standards for an ideal state? What services does it provide your community?

In what ways could your state be improved to bring its living conditions closer to those of an ideal state? What services should be provided in your community?

1. Ideal State

2. Your State

3. Potential Improvements

How Would You Improve Your State?

5. Solutions

4. Obstacles

What are some solutions to the obstacles that you found?

What are some obstacles that could prevent the changes you outlined from being instituted?

Exercise Your Mind!

Think about these questions and then use your research skills to find the answers and learn more fascinating facts about Virginia. A teacher, librarian, or parent may be able to help you locate the best sources to use in your research.

1 What natural force created Virginia's Blue Ridge region?

a. The collision of tectonic plates
b. Glaciers
c. Volcanoes
d. An earthquake

2 What is the official state folk dance of Virginia?

a. Square dance
b. Polka
c. Waltz
d. Highland dance

3 For which product is Chincoteague Island best known?

4 In which Virginia city did Patrick Henry make his "Give me liberty or give me death" speech?

5 What is the name of the area in Arlington National Cemetery that is dedicated to soldiers who lost their lives in wartime and could not be identified?

6 Which of the following is the official state beverage of Virginia?

a. Tea
b. Coffee
c. Grape juice
d. Milk

7 Which city in Virginia shares a name and main street with a city in Tennessee?

8 Which Virginia island has had wild ponies since the 1600s?

Words to Know

amphibians: animals that can live both on land and in water

archives: a collection of records and documents

broiler chickens: chickens raised for their meat rather than their eggs

civilian: a person who does not work for the military or the police

endangered: in danger of dying out

habitations: places to live

hijacked: seized by force, usually an airplane or other vehicle

indentured servants: people bound to an employer for a set number of years

metropolitan area: a large city and its surrounding towns and suburbs

plantation: large farm usually worked by people who live on the property

ratify: give formal approval

seceded: separated from an organization or nation

segregated: racially separated and restricted

steeplechase: a horse race with obstacles such as ditches and hedges

threatened: describes an animal or plant whose numbers are declining so much that it may become endangered

veto: to reject a bill passed by the legislature

Index

Log on to www.av2books.com

AV² by Weigl brings you media enhanced books that support active learning. Go to www.av2books.com, and enter the special code found on page 2 of this book. You will gain access to enriched and enhanced content that supplements and complements this book. Content includes video, audio, web links, quizzes, a slide show, and activities.

Audio
Listen to sections of the book read aloud.

Video
Watch informative video clips.

Embedded Weblinks
Gain additional information for research.

Try This!
Complete activities and hands-on experiments.

WHAT'S ONLINE?

Try This!	Embedded Weblinks	Video	EXTRA FEATURES
Test your knowledge of the state in a mapping activity.	Discover more attractions in Virginia.	Watch a video introduction to Virginia.	**Audio** Listen to sections of the book read aloud.
Find out more about precipitation in your city.	Learn more about the history of the state.	Watch a video about the features of the state.	
Plan what attractions you would like to visit in the state.	Learn the full lyrics of the state song.		**Key Words** Study vocabulary, and complete a matching word activity.
Learn more about the early natural resources of the state.			
Write a biography about a notable resident of Virginia.			**Slide Show** View images and captions, and prepare a presentation.
Complete an educational census activity.			**Quizzes** Test your knowledge.

AV² was built to bridge the gap between print and digital. We encourage you to tell us what you like and what you want to see in the future.

Sign up to be an AV² Ambassador at www.av2books.com/ambassador.